OUTRAGEOUS JOY

BIBLE STUDY FOR WOMEN

(BOOK 3)

Kimberly Taylor

TakeBackYourTemple.com

Cover Image by:

www.iStockphoto.com

Table of Contents

Introduction

Thank you for starting this third book of the *Bible Study for Women* series, *Outrageous Joy*. Scripture says that the joy of the Lord is our strength. In this 4-week study, you will learn how four women expressed joy for specific reasons: Miriam, Sarah, Elizabeth, and The Shulamite. From these examples, you will learn how you can cultivate joy in your own life.

I sometimes wonder why so many Christians lack visible joy. I once heard a quote by author and bible teacher Joyce Meyer that made me laugh: "Some people who are saved need to notify their faces."

Now that doesn't mean you have to go around with a creepy smile on your face like 'The Joker' from *Batman*. However, I do believe that our inner joy in salvation should radiant outwardly.

This reminds me of Psalm 42:11, in which the sons of Korah said:

Why are you cast down, O my soul?

And why are you disquieted within me?

Hope in God;

For I shall yet praise Him,

The help of my countenance and my God.

The psalm speaks of someone whose soul is disquieted within. In contrast, joy speaks of well-being, contentment, and internal security. You know that in spite of everything going on around you, all is well.

It's interesting that the bible mentions the word 'happy' only about 21 times, but the word 'joy' about 188 times. So many people seek happiness, yet it seems to me that joy is easier and better to obtain.

In the previous psalm, the way to joy is clear: "Hope in God." He is the ultimate source of joy and everything positive.

The apostle Paul advises in Philippians 4:8: "Finally, brethren, whatever things are true, whatever things are noble, whatever things are just, whatever things are pure, whatever things are lovely, whatever things are of good report, if there is any virtue and if there is anything praiseworthy — meditate on these things."

Your outward expression likely reflects your internal meditation.

Think about this: What are you dwelling upon most often? I recently learned that the Hebrew word for "dwell" means "to sit down." Dwell also means to "live in."

There is a difference between having negative thoughts enter your mind for a moment (you can't help that) versus choosing to "sit down" or "live" in them.

Another key to joy is also found in the psalm: "For I shall yet praise Him." That means your heart is set on praising the Lord, no matter what is happening around you.

Years ago, I used to suffer from depression frequently. But one day, the Lord led me to start an outrageous praise journal. In a blank book, I recorded seven things each day for which to praise God. I did it for 31 days consistently. I advise you to start an outrageous praise journal yourself.

Your journal should be small enough for you to carry around with you so that you can jot down your praise immediately, before you forget. As you focus on what is right in your life instead of what is wrong, you will find much more than seven things per day for which to praise God.

By the end of the 31 days, you should have a minimum of 217 things for which you are grateful to God. If you like, you can keep the journal longer. Praise is a simple way to practice God's presence. Every time you praise Him, you can be sure that He is close by and is listening.

Mentally note your attitude before the 31 days of outrageous praise compared to afterwards. Your joy in salvation will likely reflect on your face more.

Now because you are reading a bible study, I am assuming that you already have a relationship with God through accepting Jesus Christ as your Savior. But in case you don't have one yet, here is a resource about establishing a relationship with God through Jesus Christ. You can also use this resource as a means to re-dedicate your life to Christ:

http://www.everystudent.com/features/gettingc onnected.html

Are you ready to learn more about how women experienced outrageous joy in the bible? Let's get started!

How to Get the Most from this Study

The aim for each study in the *Bible Study for Women* series is to keep it simple. I want the lessons in the bible to change your life. To that end, it should be helpful to know how the lessons are organized and what you need to make the most of your study time.

Within each week's lesson, you will find:

- *Focus Scriptures* to memorize related to the current topic

- *Lesson Insight* that discusses the week's story in depth

- *Speak the WORD* affirmations that confirm your identity in Christ

- *Aim for Change* that provides questions for further reflection and discussion

To start the study, you need to have:

- *A bible:* I recommend the *New King James Version* or the *New American Standard Bible* for readability. I believe that it is important to use a bible translation that you understand for private study.

- *Index cards:* These will come in handy to write focus scriptures on so that you can 'feed' on them throughout the day.

- *A small notebook or journal:* This will enable you to keep track of the blessings/lessons you are learning as a result of this study.

- *A heart and mind that is open to the Holy Spirit's teaching:* One of the Holy Spirit's roles in the believer's life is that of *Teacher* (John 14:26). Invite Him through prayer to show you plainly the lesson God wants to teach you before you begin each study session. Be attentive to the still small voice within that prompts you to take action on the word you are learning about.

- *A commitment and willingness to give yourself grace:* If you find yourself forgetting to study as you planned, don't beat yourself up. Just start your study where you left off at your next opportunity. Think "forward motion" and keep going!

Week 1: Joy in Victory (Miriam)

Focus Scripture

> *"The Lord is my strength and song, And He has become my salvation; He is my God, and I will praise Him; My father's God, and I will exalt Him."*

- Exodus 15:2

Lesson Insight

When God performed one of the most awesome miracles in the bible, Miriam the prophetess was there. The sister of Moses, she was one of the thousands of Hebrews who walked on dry land when God parted the Red Sea miraculously so that the Israelites could escape the Egyptian army.

Moses might not have been able to fulfill his destiny if it had not been for the quick thinking actions of Miriam as a child (see Exodus 2:1-10).

Because the Egyptians feared the Hebrew slaves' population growth, Pharaoh ordered that all male Hebrew babies be thrown into the river. So when Moses' mother Jochebed gave birth to him, she at first hid her child for three months. But when she couldn't hide him any longer, she created an ark of bulrushes and made the vessel watertight with asphalt and pitch. She then placed her baby in the floating vessel and set it in the reeds by the river.

I can't imagine how heartbreaking it must have been for this mother to do this, leaving her baby not knowing what would happen to him. However, Miriam did not leave. She watched the ark, apparently from a concealed position, to see what would happen to the baby.

Soon, Pharaoh's daughter came to the river to bathe and she spotted the ark. When she opened it and saw it was a Hebrew baby, she had compassion. Miriam quickly took advantage of the moment and presented herself to Pharaoh's daughter, "Shall I go and call a nurse for you from the Hebrew women, that she may nurse the child for you?"

Pharaoh's daughter said 'yes' and Miriam went home to get her mother. Not only was Jochebed given her son

back to nurse, but Pharaoh's daughter paid her to do it!
A blessing if there ever was one.

Now nearly 80 years later, Moses had become the
deliverer of Israel. God performed great miracles
through him and Miriam witnessed most of them.
Pharaoh released the Hebrews from slavery after God
visited the 10 plagues upon Egypt.

But then Pharaoh changed his mind. And sent the entire
Egyptian army after the Hebrews.

So now they were trapped with the Red Sea in front of
them and the Egyptian army behind them.
Understandably, they were afraid.

But God had a plan, which He relayed to Moses: "...Why
do you cry to Me? Tell the children of Israel to go
forward. But lift up your rod, and stretch out your hand
over the sea and divide it. And the children of Israel
shall go on dry ground through the midst of the sea.
And I indeed will harden the hearts of the Egyptians,
and they shall follow them. So I will gain honor over
Pharaoh and over all his army, his chariots, and his
horsemen. Then the Egyptians shall know that I am the
Lord, when I have gained honor for Myself over
Pharaoh, his chariots, and his horsemen."

Events happened exactly as the Lord said; when Moses, Miriam, and the other Hebrews crossed the Red Sea on dry land, the Egyptian army followed them.

When the last Hebrews had safely crossed, the Lord directed Moses to raise His staff over the sea again. And the sea returned to its full depth with the Egyptian army in it. The army drowned; not one of them was left.

The children of Israel celebrated this miraculous victory with song. Miriam led all of the women with a timbrel, which is the modern equivalent of a tambourine.

The other women got their timbrels as well and joined her with dances to celebrate the victory.

Miriam sang, "Sing to the LORD, For He has triumphed gloriously!" This reminds me of a scripture from 1 Chronicles 16:23, "Sing to the LORD, all the earth; Proclaim the good news of His salvation from day to day."

We may not have experienced an event as miraculous as the Red Sea crossing, but we still have a perpetual reason to celebrate: Our salvation in Jesus Christ.

If you ever lack joy, then just consider that Jesus has overcome the world. Through his sacrificial death on the cross and resurrection, He conquered sin for all time. Take a cue from Miriam, singing and dancing to celebrate the Lord. In Him, we have the victory.

Speak the WORD

Speak this affirmation out loud as often as possible, based on this week's study:

> "Lord, you are my strength and salvation. I praise you with everything within me. Your goodness puts a song in my heart and a smile on my lips. I celebrate my salvation from day to day."

Aim For Change

Read Exodus 2:1-10 and Exodus 15:1-20 and then answer the following questions.

1. What relation was Miriam to Moses?

2. Why was Moses' life in danger as a baby?

3. How did Miriam's actions as a child impact Moses' destiny?

4. What miraculous event did Miriam and all the Israelites personally experience during their escape from Egypt?

5. How did Miriam and the other women celebrate their joy in victory?

6. Has there been an event in your life in which the Lord showed Himself strong in the victory?

7. How can you celebrate your salvation from day to day?

Week 2: Joy in Promises Fulfilled (Sarah)

Focus Scripture

"God has made me laugh, and all who hear will laugh with me."

- Genesis 21:6

Lesson Insight

God gave Sarah at least two occasions to laugh; the first was the promise that Sarah would deliver a son in her old age. The second was when that promise was fulfilled.

Most of us are familiar with God's promise to Abram that his descendants would be as numerous as the stars. At that point, Abram didn't have one child, plus he was old. Still, Abram believed God and God counted that belief in His promise as righteousness (see Genesis 15:1-6).

Sarai (at that point, her name had not yet been changed to Sarah) decided that since she was barren, she would obtain children in a different way. She told Abram to "please" go in to her Egyptian maid, Hagar so that Hagar would conceive and bear a child (see Genesis, chapter 16).

Abram did not protest; Hagar did become pregnant and had a son named Ishmael. However, this was not the child that God had promised. Because Abram and Sarai tried to make things happen on their own timetable, it caused much drama in the family.

Now Abram was 86 when Ishmael was born; the Lord did not appear to Abram again until he was 99 years old! At that time, God made a covenant with Abram and changed his name to *Abraham*, affirming him as the father of many nations (see Genesis, chapter 17).

Not only that, but God told Abraham that Sarai's name would be changed to *Sarah* and that He would give Abraham a son by her. She would be the mother of many nations. At that time, Sarah was 90 years old.

When Abraham heard that he fell on his face and laughed and said in his heart, "Shall a child be born to a man who is one hundred years old? And shall Sarah, who is ninety years old, bear a child?"

The Lord assured Abraham that Sarah would indeed have a son and that son should be called 'Issac.' God would establish His covenant with Issac.

Sometime later, the Lord visited Abraham again and he was given a message, this time within Sarah's hearing, "I will certainly return to you according to the time of life, and behold, Sarah your wife shall have a son."

When Sarah heard that, she laughed too: "After I have grown old, shall I have pleasure, my lord being old also?"

At this point, the Lord shows his sense of humor: "Why did Sarah laugh, saying, 'Shall I surely bear a child, since I am old?' Is anything too hard for the Lord? At the appointed time I will return to you, according to the time of life, and Sarah shall have a son."

But Sarah was afraid and denied it, saying, "I did not laugh."

However the Lord called her on it, "No, but you did laugh!" And He had the last laugh. Events happened just as God had said. Abraham and Sarah called the name of the child "Issac." The Hebrew translation of His name might make you smile:

He laughs.

When Issac was born, Sarah said "God has made me laugh, and all who hear will laugh with me."

Sarah's story tells me that God loves to do the impossible. He withholds no good thing from those who love him. So when you are faced with a seemingly impossible situation, then laugh knowing that nothing is too hard for our God.

Another reason for us to experience joy is the promises of God in the bible. The scriptures in 2 Peter 1:3-4 say, "as His divine power has given to us all things that pertain to life and godliness, through the knowledge of Him who called us by glory and virtue, by which have been given to us exceedingly great and precious promises, that through these you may be partakers of the divine nature, having escaped the corruption that is in the world through lust."

Through the promises of God, you can be all God wants you to be, do all God wants you to do, and have all God wants you to have. Take time each day to spend time in the bible so that you can discover these promises.

Like Sarah, you will discover that promises fulfilled is indeed cause for laughter and celebration.

Speak the WORD

Speak this affirmation out loud as often as possible, based on this week's study:

> "Lord, thank you for your gift of laughter. Your word says that a merry heart does good like a medicine. Meditating on your goodness makes my heart merry, so I do so at every opportunity. I am grateful for your promises, God. I am hungry for your word and search it diligently to discover your promises for me."

Aim For Change

Read Genesis 17, Genesis 18:1-18, and Genesis 21:1-6 and then answer the following questions.

1. What was the promise that God initially made to Abram?

2. How did Abram and Sarai try to make this promise occur on their own?

3. When God told Abraham that he would have a child by Sarah, what was his reaction?

4. What question did the Lord ask when Sarah laughed at his statement?

5. The Lord told Sarah and Abraham to name their child "Issac." Why do you suppose the Lord picked that name?

6. Have you ever faced a situation that seemed impossible but God came through for you? What was it?

7. How can you take advantage of God's gift of laughter every day?

Week 3: Joy in the Holy Spirit (Elizabeth)

Focus Scripture

"for the kingdom of God is not eating and drinking, but righteousness and peace and joy in the Holy Spirit."

- Romans 14:17

Lesson Insight

Like the previous account of Sarah, the story of Elizabeth is one of a woman who was once barren, but God blessed her with a child. For Sarah, her son Issac was one of the Hebrew patriarchs, the child of promise; Elizabeth's son John became the prophet sent to prepare the way for Jesus Christ.

It was John of whom Jesus said: "Assuredly, I say to you, among those born of women there has not risen one greater than John the Baptist (Matthew 11:11)"

The bible speaks well of John's parents. John's father, Zacharias, was a priest and his mother Elizabeth was of the daughters of Aaron, referring to the tribe of Levi. Of their character, it was said, "...And they were both righteous before God, walking in all the commandments and ordinances of the Lord blameless (Luke 1:6)."

When I read about the character of this couple, I immediately thought of Psalm 84:11, which promises "For the LORD God is a sun and shield; The LORD will give grace and glory; No good thing will He withhold From those who walk uprightly."

Sounds to me like this couple qualified for good things!

As Zacharias was serving in his priestly duties in the temple, an angel appeared to him, standing on the right side of the altar of incense (see Luke 1:8-25).

I wondered if there was significance to where the angel appeared to Zacharias. In my research, I discovered that incense is synonymous with prayer. In Revelation 8:3, we are given a heavenly vision: "Then another angel, having a golden censer, came and stood at the altar. He was given much incense, that he should offer it with the prayers of all the saints upon the golden altar which was before the throne."

Apparently, angels are an impressive sight. Whenever an account is given of a person seeing one in the bible, it seems they almost always experienced fear. And that is the reaction that Zacharias had.

But the angel had good news for him, "Do not be afraid, Zacharias, for your prayer is heard; and your wife Elizabeth will bear you a son, and you shall call his name John. And you will have joy and gladness, and many will rejoice at his birth. For he will be great in the sight of the Lord, and shall drink neither wine nor strong drink. He will also be filled with the Holy Spirit, even from his mother's womb. And he will turn many of the children of Israel to the Lord their God. He will also go before Him in the spirit and power of Elijah,' to turn the hearts of the fathers to the children,' and the disobedient to the wisdom of the just, to make ready a people prepared for the Lord."

So not only did the angel tell Zacharias that he would have a son, but gave him instructions from the Lord as to what his name would be as well as the child's destiny. What an awesome message!

But Zacharias apparently had doubts about whether the message was true because he said to the angel, "How shall I know this? For I am an old man, and my wife is well advanced in years."

I found it interesting that instead of immediately expressing joy at the angel's pronouncement, Zacharias' first reaction was doubt. The angel began his message by telling Zacharias that his prayer had been heard; it makes me wonder how long it had been since Zacharias had prayed for the child! If it had been recently, then may have been easier for him to believe that his prayer had been answered.

But my thought is that Zacharias prayed for the child while he and Elizabeth were younger. As the years passed and no child came, perhaps Zacharias doubted that God even heard the prayer. Once Elizabeth passed childbearing age, he likely gave up the possibility of it ever happening.

Zacharias' question apparently displeased the Lord because the angel replied, "I am Gabriel, who stands in the presence of God, and was sent to speak to you and bring you these glad tidings. But behold, you will be mute and not able to speak until the day these things take place, because you did not believe my words which will be fulfilled in their own time."

Wow. Imagine having an amazing experience like that and not be able to speak to anyone about it! When he came out of the temple, all Zacharias could do was motion to the people to communicate with them.

24

When Zacharias went home, he was intimate with his wife Elizabeth and she conceived. But Elizabeth hid herself for five months saying that the Lord has taken away her reproach among people. In ancient times, people viewed barrenness as a punishment from God. They thought there must be a reason that He withheld children from a woman. But God is sovereign; in Elizabeth and Zacharias' case, he had determined exactly when John the Baptist needed to be born into the world.

Most of us know that the same angel who appeared before Zacharias, Gabriel, was sent to Mary to announce that she would conceive the Messiah. When Gabriel made the announcement to Mary, I found it interesting that Mary's response to him was similar to Zacharias': "How can this be, since I do not know a man?"

And yet, Gabriel did not make Mary mute! Did Zacharias just catch Gabriel on a bad day?

But when I looked at the statements more closely, I realized that Zacharias asked, "How shall I know this?" His statement implied that he wanted the angel to prove it to him, to give him a sign that things would happen as he said.

However, Mary's question: "How can this be" speaks of curiosity. She doesn't doubt that it could happen; she just wondered **how it would happen!**

Gabriel patiently explained how events would happen and they transpired exactly the way the Lord ordained.

Sometime later, Mary went to visit Elizabeth her cousin. And when Mary entered the house, and greeted Elizabeth, John leaped in Elizabeth's womb and Elizabeth was filled with the Holy Spirit.

She proclaimed: "Blessed are you among women, and blessed is the fruit of your womb! But why is this granted to me, that the mother of my Lord should come to me? For indeed, as soon as the voice of your greeting sounded in my ears, the babe leaped in my womb for joy. Blessed is she who believed, for there will be a fulfillment of those things which were told her from the Lord."

Elizabeth's words to Mary tell me that in order to see fulfillment of God's promises, there must first be belief.

Elizabeth also said to Mary, "Blessed is the fruit of your womb!" Did you know that you have fruit in *your* Spiritual womb? Yes, you are pregnant! Every believer in Christ Jesus has the Holy Spirit inside of them. John 16:13-15 says:

> "However, when He, the Spirit of truth, has come, He will guide you into all truth; for He will not speak on His own authority, but whatever He hears He will speak; and He will tell you things to come. He will glorify Me, for He will take of what is Mine and declare it to you. All things that the Father has are Mine. Therefore I said that He will take of Mine and declare it to you."

What can prevent you from allowing the Spirit of God to guide you? It is the condition of your heart. You must set your heart on yielding to the Spirit's leading and direction. If you are having difficulty in this area, then pray that God give you a new heart.

You know that you are yielded to the Spirit because the Spirit's fruit will be cultivated in you. Are you growing in love, joy, peace, patience, kindness, goodness, faithfulness, gentleness and self-control? This is not an overnight process, so you must be patient - just like growing a baby in the natural.

If you allow patience to do its work, then the bible says that you will be complete and lack nothing.

Most of all, you will not lack joy. Then someday others can taste your Spiritual fruit and know that the Lord is good!

Speak the WORD

Speak this affirmation out loud as often as possible, based on this week's study:

> "Lord, I am thankful that your Holy Spirit leads me and guides me. He teaches me all truth and tells me things to come. As I submit to the Holy Spirit's leading, I grow in righteousness, peace, and joy every day."

Aim For Change

Read Luke 1:5-25. Then answer the following questions.

1. How was Elizabeth and Zacharias' character described in the bible?

2. What did the angel tell Zacharias' about his son that would be conceived?

3. How did Zacharias respond to the news?

4. When Elizabeth discovered that she had conceived, how did she respond?

5. When Mary visited Elizabeth and she heard Mary's greeting, what happened?

6. Meditate a moment on the following scripture regarding the fruit of Spirit in Galatians 5:22-23: "But the fruit of the Spirit is love, joy, peace, longsuffering, kindness, goodness, faithfulness, gentleness, self-control. Against such there is no law."

7. Think about each of the fruits mentioned. Since you accepted Jesus as your Savior, are you growing in Spiritual fruit? If you are not growing, then submit this concern to the Lord in prayer and your desire to glorify Him in the fruit you bear. He will honor this request.

Week 4: Joy in Loving Relationship (The Shulamite)

Focus Scripture

We will be glad and rejoice in you. We will remember your love more than wine.

- Song of Solomon 1:4

Lesson Insight

The Song of Solomon is the most passionate book in the whole bible. Some bible scholars say that the series of poems show God's picture of the ideal marriage relationship; others say that it is metaphorical, expressing the relationship of Jesus Christ with the church.

In my opinion, it is both. Clearly, Solomon did exist and he loved a woman he affectionately called 'The Shulamite.' The love and respect demonstrated in the song reflects what most of us long to experience in our relationships, especially with the Creator who knows us best.

Throughout the song, you get varying views of the relationship - the bridegroom's, the bride's, the community (the Daughters of Jerusalem) and the relatives (the bride's brothers). The bridegroom refers to his bride as "my love" and the bride refers to her bridegroom "my beloved."

Let's take a closer look at the relationship from the Shulamite's perspective. Here are some of her viewpoints:

Let him kiss me with the kisses of his mouth—

For your love is better than wine.

Because of the fragrance of your good ointments,

Your name is ointment poured forth;

Therefore the virgins love you.

Draw me away! (see Song of Solomon 1:2-4)

The heat is on! When I read this, I could sense the Shulamite's desire for her beloved's presence. She is intoxicated with his love for her. When she speaks of his "good ointments" and compares his name to ointment, my interpretation is that his presence is healing to her. One of the traditional names titles given to Jesus is "a balm in Gilead."

This name comes from Jeremiah 8:22 in which the prophet asks, "Is there no balm in Gilead, Is there no physician there? Why then is there no recovery For the health of the daughter of my people?" We know that man has a terminal illness - sin. The only cure for that sin was the sacrifice Jesus made for us. He was the ultimate physician and healer.

> Tell me, O you whom I love,
>
> Where you feed your flock,
>
> Where you make it rest at noon.
>
> For why should I be as one who veils herself
>
> By the flocks of your companions? (see Song of Solomon 1:7)

In this passage, the Shulamite is actively seeking her beloved. She wants to completely reveal herself to him. Is it not the desire of the human heart - to know another as you are known? God promises in Jeremiah

29:13: "And you will seek Me and find Me, when you search for Me with all your heart."

Behold, you are handsome, my beloved!

Yes, pleasant!

Also our bed is green.

The beams of our houses are cedar,

And our rafters of fir. (see Song of Solomon 1:16-17)

In this passage, you sense the Shulamite's appreciation for her beloved's appearance. And then she comments on the state of their relationship. When she says their bed is green, she is referring to the intimacy of their relationship - it is fresh and flourishing. In addition, Shulamite sees their relationship as solid; she compares it to the cedar beams of a house. This wood is not only strong, but it is also fragrant and naturally resistant to termites and rot.

The Shulamite is recognizing the value of a protecting her relationship - she does those things that keep her relationship strong on a daily basis. She affirms her high regard for her beloved; she does not take him for granted but appreciates his strengths. When you "appreciate" someone, you add value to them.

Like an apple tree among the trees of the woods,

So is my beloved among the sons.

I sat down in his shade with great delight,

And his fruit was sweet to my taste. (see Song of Solomon 2:3)

When the Shulamite talks of sitting down in her beloved's shade, I think of the promise of rest in Jesus Christ. We no longer have to strive to be accepted by Him, we can rest secure in His finished work. In addition, the passage refers to the fruit of the beloved. In the previous week, we discussed the fruit of the Spirit: love, joy, peace, patience, kindness, goodness, faithfulness, gentleness, and self control. The Shulamite expresses her enjoyment of the beloved's fruit. Implicit in this is her desire for more.

His mouth is most sweet,

Yes, he is altogether lovely.

This is my beloved,

And this is my friend,

O daughters of Jerusalem! (see Song of Solomon 5:16)

Looking at this from a metaphorical perspective, I think of the beloved's mouth in conjunction with the words He speaks. Throughout the song, the couple speaks words of life to each other. They complement each other on their appearances and character, re-assuring each other of their desire and value to the other.

The Shulamite says that her beloved is also her friend; that means she not only views him in a romantic light, but she also trusts him as her confidant and companion. Oh how joyous to have a friend in Jesus! He is the lover of our soul and meets every need we will ever have.

Speak the WORD

Speak this affirmation out loud as often as possible, based on this week's study:

> Lord, I rejoice in you. I remember that your love is greater than anything I possess. You are my beloved, my Savior, and my friend.

Aim For Change

Read Song of Solomon, Chapters 1, 2, and 5 and then answer the following questions.

1. To what did the Shulamite compare Solomon's love? Why do you think she made this comparison?

2. To what did the Shulamite compare her Beloved's name? Why do you think she made this comparison?

3. What comparisons did the Shulamite make to describe her relationship with the Beloved?

4. What do you think the Shulamite meant when she spoke of resting in the Beloved's shade?

5. How did the Shulamite summarize her relationship with the Beloved?

6. In reading these passages from the Song of Solomon, what are some of the common themes in how the Shulamite and her Beloved relate to one another?

7. Think about your relationship with Jesus Christ. Do you have the passion for his presence as in

the Song? If not, how can you cultivate this relationship?

Study Summary

In the *Outrageous Joy* bible study, you were reminded that the joy of the Lord is our strength. So you learned it is important to cultivate joy in your life. I suggested that you start a '31 days of outrageous praise' journal in which you strive to write down seven things each day for which you want to praise God.

Regarding the bible passages discussed, you learned how four women expressed joy for specific reasons: Miriam, Sarah, Elizabeth, and The Shulamite. From these examples, you learned how you can cultivate joy in your own life.

Points to Remember

- If you ever lack joy, then just consider that Jesus has overcome the world. Through his sacrificial death on the cross and resurrection, He conquered sin. Sing and dance to celebrate the Lord. In Him, we have the victory.

- God loves to do the impossible. He withholds no good thing from those who love him. So you can laugh when you are faced with a seemingly impossible situation, knowing that nothing is too hard for our God. Another reason for you to experience joy is the promises of God in the bible. Take time each day to spend time in the bible so that you can discover these promises.

- As a believer, the Holy Spirit dwells within you and one of the fruits of the Spirit is joy. The fruit grows the more you are yielded to the Holy Spirit's leading. Ask yourself: Am I growing in love, joy, peace, patience, kindness, goodness, faithfulness, gentleness and self-control? This is not an overnight process, so you must be patient.

- The joy in relationship comes from the appreciation of the other's value. In intimate relationships, you value your spouse as a lover, confidant, and companion. In a similar way, you value the relationship you have in Jesus. He meets every need you will ever have.

About the Author

"Just wanted to again thank you for sharing your unique and engaging presentation to help us take back our temples! You were truly a blessing and I know that many were enlightened by what you shared."

- Danese Turner, Turner Chapel AME, Marietta GA

Kimberly Taylor is the creator of **Takebackyourtemple.com**, a website that inspires Christians to Spiritual, emotional, and physical health. She is the author of the ebook *Take Back Your Temple* and the books ***The Weight Loss Scriptures***, ***God's Word is Food***, and **many others**.

Once 240 pounds and a size 22, Kim lost 85 pounds through renewing her mind and taking action upon God's word. Her experience led her to establish the **Take Back Your Temple** website. "Take Back Your Temple" is a prayer that asks God to take control of your body and your life so He can use them for His purpose and agenda.

Kim's weight loss success story has been featured on CBN's *The 700 Club,* and in *Prevention Magazine, Essence Magazine, Charisma Magazine* and many other magazines and newspapers. She has also been interviewed on various radio programs.

Kim exhorts people of faith to become good stewards of all the resources God has given to them, including time, money, talents, and physical health. "I am passionate about empowering others to adopt healthy lifestyles so they can fulfill their God-given purpose," she says.

"My dream is for God's people to stand apart because we are healthy, prosperous and living the abundant life to which we are called. I want non-believers to look at us and want what we have: Spiritual, mental, and physical wholeness. Then when they ask us what we are doing differently, we can tell them about Jesus, the author and finisher of our faith."

Stay Connected

You can stay connected with Kimberly Taylor through the following channels:

Amazon Author Page

You can learn about all of Kimberly Taylor's books and eBooks available on Amazon.com at one convenient location:
https://www.amazon.com/author/kimberlyytaylor

Take Back Your Temple website

Kimberly's website, **www.takebackyourtemple.com/** shares her testimony of deliverance from emotional overeating through the change God made in her heart and mind. Hundreds of free articles on the website encourage other Christians on the road to Spiritual, emotional, and physical health.

YouTube

Kimberly is creating a *Bible Study for Women* channel with videos that discuss her insights on women of the bible. The channel address is **http://www.youtube.com/user/BibleStudyforWomen1** (Available September 11, 2012)

Facebook

You can connect with Kimberly on Facebook at **http://www.facebook.com/takebackyourtemple**. She also moderates a secret Facebook support group comprised of believers who struggle with emotional eating and are working to change their health. Details on how to join the group are available at *takebackyourtemple.com*.

Twitter

Follow Kimberly on Twitter at **twitter.com/tbytkimberly**

Pinterest

You can view Kim's Pinterest boards at
http://pinterest.com/tbyt/

All paperback versions of the *Bible Study for Women* series were published through **CreateSpace**.

3234919R00026

Printed in Great Britain
by Amazon.co.uk, Ltd.,
Marston Gate.